Jeff Bowick & Dwayne Henriksen

TRADING STRATEGIES AND SECRETS: CRYPTO TRADING

A very useful guide to start investing in Bitcoin and other Cryptocurrencies

Table of Contents

INTRODUCTION

Today, is investing in cryptocurrencies an opportunity or a risk? This is what millions of people around the world are asking themselves when they see the new records set by virtual currencies in terms of quotations and it is normal to wonder if they are not missing a great opportunity or if investing in this field does not represent a risk to be avoided.

Already the word investment can sometimes even scare you, but if you turn to the right sector and assets the word invest can only sound as sweet as music.

So what we're going to do here is try to figure out whether or not it's worth investing in cryptocurrencies. Don't miss this guide because in addition to clarifying whether or not it is profitable we will also talk about the individual virtual currencies currently in circulation to understand how they are doing and which of them could know a boom in these times or in the near future.

At the moment there are more than 2.186 virtual currencies (with a capitalization of more than 228 billion dollars) in circulation and they are not few, it's impossible to know all of them but there are some to which we must pay great attention, both on the markets and for a possible landing in the real economy.

At this moment, the thing that is clearer is that very few people know the world of virtual currencies and even less really understand how they work. This implies a lower liquidity than if there were more investors, but at the same time opens to the careful investor opportunities to trade cryptocurrencies without the disturbance of a strong competition.

The media itself is not giving much prominence to the potential of blockchain and its developments, moreover since the birth of bitcoin many have been led to think that this system would be just a meteor that would soon fade away, but this was not the case and you only have to look at today's data to understand this given the current market price of bitcoin which is really exorbitant and no one expected it.

So, investing in cryptocurrencies can be a great solution, but it is good to keep in mind that, being a form of investment, like all other forms of investment involves inevitable risks. Risks that are other and different than those of traditional markets and that must be known.

In this book we will talk about cryptocurrencies, the best known strategies and forms of investment through them and also the risks involved in this activity in order to give you a picture as clear and complete as possible of what awaits you.

THE MOST IMPORTANT CRYPTOCURRENCIES

If you can overcome the clichés related to beliefs about cryptocurrencies, investing in them is a respectable and really convenient activity. It is no coincidence that these are now considered by many investors as a formidable asset and there are already those who regret not having thought before.

If we look at the numbers it is clear that all traders who in the past have bought bitcoins for example, have now accumulated a fortune because their value has skyrocketed for a long time. Only that once they were not worth anything and therefore few have believed in them.

So here are the 5 virtual currencies that are worth investing in right now:

Bitcoin (BTC)

The first and most important cryptocurrency by market capitalization. It was created in 2009 by an inventor whose identity is unknown, who uses the pseudonym Satoshi Nakamoto.

BitCoin, can be defined as a cryptocurrency to invest in. Nothing more obvious given that the BTC has recently reached a high price compared to the beginning of his career coming today to touch $ 7800 but analysts predict a strong overvaluation for the next few years with peaks that could touch $ 100,000 and more.

Bitcoin is collecting record figures in the latest cryptocurrency quotes

As you can see by following the financial news, bitcoin has been growing continuously for about 3 years. But we also want to mention that the adoption rate of all cryptocurrencies has reached this point thanks mainly to the Bitcoin trailblazer.

Bitcoins, we know, are considered as the cryptocurrency par excellence and it is to these that the majority of other cryptocurrencies owe their existence. Without the mistakes that Bitcoin had to experience first, the others would not have been able to come up with a mechanism as sophisticated and advanced as the one we all know today. In the future, bitcoins can still be a big deal for investors.

Ethereum (ETHEREUM)

The right definition would be Ether, since Ethereum is the system, but now common practice refers to this currency as Ethereum.

It was created by Russian programmer, Vitalik Buterin, and launched in 2015.

At this moment it is the second most important virtual currency and comes right after Bitcoin, this is mainly due to its capitalization which is largely due to the help of large international companies such as Microsoft and Intel.

The strength of this currency is that it is based on a new concept of blockchain useful for the exchange of any kind of value directly on the network.

In addition to payments, Ethereum also supports "smart contracts".

So that's why large multinational organizations have never lost sight of the development of Ethereum and this will not happen even in the coming years when the coin will continue to grow, so our advice is to monitor the situation and think seriously about trading on Ethereum with the best online brokers.

Ripple by Ripple Labs (XRP)

The third virtual currency we want to talk about is Ripple.

Launched in 2012 by Ripple Labs, a company founded by American programmer Jed McCaleb

XRP enables real-time payments and transactions with greater speed and lower costs and allows the exchange of its tokens without charging a fee. Upstream there is an organization that is considered one of the most professional and reliable.

Ripple, however, has also undergone strong fluctuations in the past, which led to the value of 10k satoshi, and then go down again and be traded on a value between 800 and 1000 satoshi. Lately, however, the volume of trade is intensifying.

In 2007 Ripple was back on the scene. Today you can see that the value compared to BTC is quite low. However, it is not ruled out that this currency may soon return to be considered as the first alternative to BTC.

It aims to provide solutions to financial institutions and XRP is already used by many famous banks, such as Bank of America and UBS.

Litecoin (LTC)

It was launched in 2011 by former Google engineer Charles Lee.

Litecoin is based on Bitcoin's technology, but it offers faster processing times and a larger number of coins.

It was the first cryptocurrency to implement SegWit, a method of speeding up transaction times without compromising the underlying blockchain technology

This currency was initially considered as an alternative to BitCoin for quite some time, not least because it had been scoring high rates in 2013. Following this success, however, its decline was witnessed and it failed to maintain its initial momentum.

Adding to this is the fact that the emergence of other cryptocurrencies has slowed down the race of this coin. Its initial value is $67. Today, however, it is listed at around $4. Despite everything, however, it is easy to see that Litecoin is still the most widely used.

For its usage it is second only to Bitcoin, in most of the websites that accept virtual currency payments. Contrary to everything you may think, the organization is solid and there is no question about the professionalism of the developers who support the LTC. On the basis of these considerations, it is not difficult to say that Litecoin can make a strong comeback even after a period spent in silence.

Monero

Last among the 5 but only by capitalization, we have Monero. This cryptocurrency, is considered as the virtual currency of the moment having gone from a valuation of about $1 at the beginning of June 2016 to being worth about $7.5 at the end of November 2016.

Many traders love to speculate on it. This type of investment has led the Monero to be worth $120. This is also due to the fame it has earned in being the most anonymous cryptocurrency.

There is also to say that the Monero team has announced the development of payb.ee, which is nothing but a useful gateway for payments and would allow instant conversion between Monero, Bitcoin and fiat currencies.

If all this is brought to fruition, there would be a massive adoption of Monero by both traders and also merchants.

All of which would lead to a rise in the price, all the way to very high levels, even higher than the current ones. For this reason, Monero is considered a cryptocurrency with very high potential and is for many an investment not to be missed.

In addition to these super cryptocurrencies, there are many others, all of which have great potential and, therefore, should be kept under constant observation. Let's see them together.

Ethereum Classic (ETC)

Created in 2016, when Ethereum underwent a 'hard fork'

After Ethereum's founders switched to a new blockchain, the original Ethereum platform became Ethereum Classic

Ethereum Classic has a significantly lower market capitalization than its namesake, but even so it's a popular cryptocurrency

Bitcoin Cash (BCH)

Created in August 2017, when Bitcoin underwent a 'hard fork'

Designed to be a solution to the transaction delays Bitcoin was encountering

Larger block size (eight times that of Bitcoin) and improved hash value allow for faster transaction speeds at a lower cost

Dash (DASH)

Developed by software programmer Evan Duffield

Originally launched in 2014 as XCoin, renamed as Dash in 2015

Based on Bitcoin's technology, Dash's additional infrastructure allows for faster transactions and greater liquidity

Unlike other cryptocurrencies, Dash is a decentralized autonomous organization (DAO).

Stellar Lumens (XLM)

Launched in 2014 and co-founded by Jed McCaleb, the creator of Ripple

Operates on a unique consensus algorithm instead of mining

The average confirmation time for a Stellar transaction is extremely fast, completed in seconds, and at an extremely low cost. Stellar can facilitate transactions between multiple currencies, both fiat and digital

NEO (NEO).

Created in 2014 by Da Hongfei, is modeled after ETH, and is also known as "Chinese Ethereum"

Designed to be easily modified and have no fork capabilities, NEO faces fewer challenges in the Chinese market than other cryptocurrencies

NEO's total supply is limited to 100 million coins, to be put into circulation gradually.

EOS (EOS)

Launched in early 2018, EOS has quickly become one of the top ten cryptocurrencies

With similar functionality to Ethereum, EOS is designed for faster transactions and extreme scalability

EOS's powerful open source infrastructure could potentially support thousands of decentralized commercial-scale applications (DApps)

EOS uses a Delegated Proof of Stake (DPOS), rather than a mining-based blockchain

Cardano (ADA)

Launched in September 2017, Cardano quickly reached a market capitalization of several billion dollars

Inspired by Ethereum, Cardano aims to use blockchain technology for much more than simply payment processing

Allows developers to create their own blockchain apps using the platform

Cardano's dual-tier structure runs each layer separately, as opposed to Ethereum, where the two layers are interconnected

IOTA (MIOTA)

Launched in 2015

IOTA is based on a proprietary "blockless" blockchain called Tangle

Has formed strategic partnerships with well-known brands such as Volkswagen

IOTA is paving the way for using a decentralized network to power the Internet of Things (IoT)

Zcash (ZEC)

Launched in 2016

Zcash encrypts the content of screened transactions, using a new form of zero-knowledge cryptography called zk-SNARKs that verifies their validity

Ensures that both the sender and recipient and the amount transferred remain private

Zcash has a total fixed supply of 21 million units, similar to Bitcoin

Binance Coin (BNB)

First founded in Shanghai in 2017, Binance now operates from Taiwan

BNB is a utility cryptocurrency used to pay transaction exchange fees

It provides traders with a discount on the nominal 0.1% of the transaction value and supports transactions for over 150 cryptocurrencies

THE BITCOIN

Bitcoin

Bitcoin was founded in 2008 and launched the following year by a person or persons whose identity is unknown, using the alias Satoshi Nakamoto. Although it was initially only adopted by blockchain enthusiasts, the fact that it allowed users to transact quickly while maintaining anonymity caused its popularity to grow exponentially over time. The first purchase of physical goods made using Bitcoin was 10,000 BTC for two pizzas, in 2010. The same pizzas were worth $190,000,000 in January 2018.

As Bitcoin became increasingly popular, numerous other cryptocurrencies were created. Some were built on the same technology, while others created their own blockchain protocols. However, despite increasing competition in the crypto space, Bitcoin has maintained its place as the world's largest crypto by market capitalization for many years.

There are many reasons for this success as there are many advantages to trading with Bitcoins. But are Bitcoins suitable for everyone? Indeed they are.

Since it is, as we said, the most popular cryptocurrency, many crypto traders buy it as part of their cryptocurrency portfolio.

But it is also widely used by long-term investors. Although, in fact, it is still considered an extremely volatile and risky market, Bitcoin has shown exceptional price increases over time. Therefore, those who believe that the overall trend will be positive might consider an investment in Bitcoin.

Obviously, Bitcoin is very much in vogue among traders who practice various short-term strategies such as Day Trading, Swing Trading and the like. BTC prices with frequency can experience significant swings over the course of a few hours. Traders may attempt to take advantage of these movements in an effort to make a short-term profit.

Blockchain enthusiasts, who typically have confidence in the technology and its potential impact in the technology and financial sectors, have also developed a great deal of interest in Bitcoin over time since this cryptocurrency is the first major application of blockchain technology.

Bitcoin is a highly volatile instrument that has experienced huge price swings over the years, sometimes gaining hundreds of percentage points or instead losing them in a relatively short period of time. Although it is affected less than other currency markets and markets in general by events in the global economy, it can be affected by a variety of factors related to the crypto space, the blockchain industry, and regulatory issues.

For example, towards the end of 2017, the media began to talk extensively about cryptocurrencies, generating unprecedented collective interest in them. People who had previously never heard of crypto started asking how they could buy Bitcoins. This triggered a massive crypto bull run, which peaked in December 2017, when almost all major cryptos reached record highs.

Another factor that can affect the price and performance of the cryptocurrency market is the performance and volatility of conventional markets. This is a mediated influence, but still significant. The volatility of the conventional market, in fact, can generate some distrust in the investor and the same happens when there are strong declines. In these cases, the investor may turn to the crypto market as an alternative.

Although, then, cryptocurrencies are usually not touched by the rules that govern conventional markets, the trend has been to prune them within a more regulated system. In fact, over the years, there have been several attempts to introduce Bitcoin into traditional markets in the form of ETFs, futures contracts and other financial instruments. Since many of these instruments require regulatory approval, traditional regulators, such as the U.S. Securities and Exchange Commission (SEC), could have a major impact on the market, whether they approve or deny these instruments.

Bringing the public closer to the technology, then, also plays or could play a crucial role in the spread of cryptocurrencies and Bitcoin in particular.

Bitcoin and Miners

The way Bitcoin operates as a decentralized network relies on its members, some of whom are miners. Miners allocate processing capacity to make transactions and are rewarded with a small fee for each transaction. Because these processes require computing power and electricity, Bitcoin miners generally are those who have invested large sums of money to build mining computers.

However, miners have another key role. When the Bitcoin blockchain network needs to undergo a change or update, it needs the approval of its members, who can signal whether or not they approve of the change. If the change is significant, it is known as a hard fork. When there are not enough participants approving the change, a hard fork results in the creation in a parallel blockchain network.

This was the case with the hard fork of Bitcoin Cash in August 2017. With this hard fork, a group of developers intentionally submitted a protocol that they knew would be rejected by some network members, thus creating a hard fork and a new cryptocurrency. Bitcoin Cash became an incredible success, reaching a market capitalization of billions and becoming a top 5 crypto.

Bitcoin now

Bitcoin has also recently been affected by the global economic crisis.

The price of bitcoin, up about 50 percent since January to $11,400 per bitcoin, has risen in line with equity markets since a coronavirus-induced crash in March.

On its future course, a great deal of, indeed, confidence has been generated just in this last period.

A prominent Tesla investor made a bold prediction of $1 trillion in market capitalization, which ignited the bitcoin and cryptocurrency community. After him, Raoul Pal, founder and managing director of Global Macro Investor and former hedge fund manager at Goldman Sachs, said the price of bitcoin could reach $1 million in just five years - a huge 10,000% increase.

Pal revealed that he has dedicated more than 50% of his portfolio to bitcoin.

Jack Dorsey, CEO of Twitter, is an ardent bitcoin supporter and recently purchased $50 million worth of bitcoin, 1% of his cash reserves, pushing this cryptocurrency even further into the limelight.

In the wake of these statements and externals, many strong investors have begun to take a great deal of interest in bitcoins, which is evidenced by financial advisors managing their portfolios.i

Michael Novogratz, another Goldman Sachs veteran and former billionaire hedge fund manager, recently turned investor in bitcoin and cryptocurrency and recently warned Goldman that he will soon be rushing to reclaim his lead in bitcoin and cryptocurrency.

So will Bitcoins remain the kings of cryptocurrency in the years to come? The answer is difficult, but we are inclined to say yes.

In fact, since Bitcoin was the only cryptocurrency in the world, a lot has happened in the crypto industry. Growing rapidly in number, there are now thousands of cryptos, many with substantial market capitalizations and trading volumes. However, Bitcoin remains at the forefront of the industry, if for no other reason than its simple and impressive size. As the industry advances and diversifies, the possibility exists that Bitcoin will lose its place as the largest crypto. However, such a scenario seems highly unlikely in the near future, and Bitcoin could very well retain its place as the world's largest crypto for years to come.

HOW TO START: CRYPTO TRADING WITH TRADING PLATFORMS

Practice with crypto trading demo and then start with the real business. Trading demo is a valuable instrument that has many functions: as an educational tool, for training employees, to gather feedback and statistics about the system and to provide a very realistic picture of what you get when you invest in cryptos. Since it is not possible to simulate all effects in real life, trading on demo allows us to study market mechanisms and test strategies without any risk. And then you can easily make the right choice about investing in crypto.

If you want to make profits and want to be successful in cryptos, you need to know exactly what is happening in the world of new money and constantly monitor the market. No one will give you a guarantee to your investments!

Make using crypto trading demo, it will help you know more about the market and give an opportunity to work with tools that are used on real trading accounts.

To work with the demo account, you need to open a new account on our platform. We will provide you a free demo ether wallet and then make it easy for you to create a new wallet. We will help you create your own private key and then share all the possibilities of using the demo account with you so that you can use it as your regular tradings account.

You can start trading with virtual money with the help of demo account, the only condition is that you will not start with real money.

To get started with crypto trading demo you need to follow these simple steps:

Step 1: Create your trading account and make a free ether wallet.

Step 2: Choose the desired crypts from the list and make a transaction in that particular coin.

Step 3: After finishing your transaction, we will verify it.

Step 4: You will have your password and private key after the verification.

Step 5: To withdraw funds from your wallet, you need to go to the "Withdraw funds" section and see the withdrawal form.

Step 6: Enter the amount of money you want to withdraw and fill in all information required.

Step 7: Click on "Send withdrawal request" button, we will verify your details and then send money to your wallet.

Step 8: After the withdrawal is complete, it can take up to 5 minutes for money to be transferred.

Step 9: Open your trading account and make a deposit.

After the deposit is complete, you can start trading with demo account.

You will see the profits and losses in your daily reports.

You do not need to download any software, you can use it both on Windows and Mac operating systems. To start making trades, all you need to do is click buy or sell buttons and then make a transaction.

The transactions are verified automatically, which means that you will receive the amount of cryptocoins that have been ordered by the user.

You can also make a transaction deposit if you make a deposit in your demo account, then you can use the role of management of the account.

Features of the demo account:

- For beginners: a very simple and easy interface that will help you start trading.

- Because you do not need to deposit any money on your demo account, everything is free and all transactions are automatically verified, so you will get instant feedback on your activity.

- All transactions are instantly verified.

- You can manage your trades by yourself.

- The minimum deposit is 1 cent, for comparison, in real accounts you need to have at least $5.

- You can test all the functions of our platform.

- You will get a 100% profit on your deposits into the demo account.

That is why crypto trading demo is so important for you and why you should make use it. All risks are personal, there are no rules or regulations that will protect you from investing in crypto.

To invest in cryptocurrencies, you will need to use a broker. Just like traditional brokers, cryptocurrency brokers are intermediaries who put buy and sell orders from traders on their exchange. The difference is that cryptocurrency exchanges operate 24/7.

There are four main types of brokers that you should be aware of:

- fiat-crypto exchange - This is a broker that offers trading in crypto currencies both with fiat currencies (i.e. dollars or euros) and other cryptocurrencies. They are usually exchanges based in a country but they operate globally. Usually, these exchanges are more user friendly and have better customer support due to the fact that they require users to verify their identity.

- crypto-crypto exchange - This is an exchange that only facilitates trades between cryptocurrencies. If you wish to buy coins with fiat currency or trade them for another cryptocurrency, you will need to change them either on another platform or on a fiat-crypto platform.

- crypto-fiat exchange - This type of exchange allows traders to convert from crypto to fiat currencies only. Many traders use this type of broker to hedge their crypto holdings.

To start trading, you do not need any previous experience or expertise on the subject and it is much easier than traditional stock trading. All you need are a few minutes of your time, your capital (i.e. money), and an account at one of the exchanges listed above. Once you have registered with a broker, you should make sure to choose the correct platform. Since many brokers offer the same services, just like traditional stock exchanges, it is important to know what the different types of exchanges are.

I'll admit it, I've been bitten by the crypto trading bug. It's an exciting new market that seems like it's here to stay. But with all good things come bad, and there is no shortage of scams in this industry. That's why today I wanted to share some tips on what to watch out for in the cryptocurrency world and how to avoid falling victim to fraud schemes.

For those not familiar, there are several types of fraud or scams in cryptocurrency trading. These include:

Pump & Dump

This is a scam where the price of a coin is artificially inflated by coordinated buying, usually on low volume exchanges. The scammers then sell into the rise they create and profit from the resulting drop in price. Most of these pumps will occur after a listing on larger exchanges, so you will see an instant spike in price followed by a sharp drop shortly after. One way to avoid pump and dump schemes is to research the history of the coin. If the price spikes and then drops off within hours of being listed on an exchange, that's a good indication it was a pump and dump.

Scam ICOs

An ICO - Initial Coin Offering - is how new coins are sold to early investors. Sometimes these coins are legitimate but many occasions they are simple scams. Beware of coins that are suddenly being covered by mainstream media, or coins that seem too good to be true.

The Mad Scientist

To avoid falling into the trap of the scam ICO, you should always follow this rule: "If it's too good to be true, it probably is." There are many (usually) legitimate ICOs out there, but be sure to do your research before investing in any new coin.

Etherium Parody

Another type of scam is the spoof, which happens when a coin's real name and logo are used but the project itself is fake. The recent Etherium fiasco is a perfect example of this. Remember, there's often more than meets the eye when it comes to legitimate projects.

Avoid FOMO

One of the risks in any type of trading is letting fear of missing out (FOMO) affect your investment decisions. If you see a coin that was just added to the top exchange, which is pumping and dumping, and that has an incredible ROI - Return on Investment - this is a sign the coin is likely one of these scams. FOMO can also play a role in ICO investing, especially if there's a lot of hype around certain projects. Avoid hyped currencies that receive tons of FOMO after they hit an exchange.

The "whale"

Some of the biggest pump and dump and scam ICOs are brought about by a single or group of investors who buy in bulk at lower prices, then reap the benefits of a rise in price. These whales are usually individuals with massive amounts of capital and knowledge about the market, and their identities are carefully guarded.

Crypto Copy Trading

Copy trading enables investors to mimic the actions of other traders, with minimal risk, but is subject to broker price risks. This means that if another trader loses money, you could lose money as well if you don't exit with a loss before your broker sells coins at a loss.

TRADING CRYPTO: EXCHANGES

Now the important question to be solved is more about HOW to invest in cryptocurrencies and therefore which instruments to use.

There are two ways to practice cryptocurrency trading: buying or selling cryptocurrencies on exchanges or buying and selling cryptocurrencies in online cfd trading.

The first way to invest in cryptocurrencies with Exchanges involves more direct operations with digital currencies by the investor.

Once identified a good Exchange with a positive reputation on the network, it is necessary to proceed to a first registration enclosing in case also personal documents for identity verification and choose a Wallet on which to make payments.

Among the merits of the Exchange, the low cost of commission to buy or sell cryptocurrencies in a direct way thanks to a greater liquidity.

Among the drawbacks, however, there is the risk of fraud: we urge you to be very careful in the online registration phase to avoid scams from Exchange momentary and not solid. However, this limitation is easily overcome by direct research on the web channels.

But how exactly do you invest with exchanges?

To invest in cryptocurrencies with exchanges, you must first choose the platform on which to operate and be able to exchange cryptocurrencies in real currency (the main exchange currencies are Dollar and Euro) or cryptocurrencies with other cryptocurrencies (Bitcoin is the main reference virtual currency). After a first phase of online registration and sending of personal documents, you can then proceed with the actual investment.

There are two main advantages of this solution, the low commission costs to carry out direct trading operations on the best cryptocurrencies and also exchange them in real currency or the high liquidity of the aforementioned cryptocurrencies. Furthermore, online security and offline data processing are among the top priorities of exchanges for investing in cryptocurrencies.

The best solutions for investing in cryptocurrencies through exchanges are undoubtedly Binance or Coinbase, which are among the most sought after and used in the world thanks to the quality of the services offered to the customer and the honest commissions.

TRADING CRYPTO WITH CFD

You've heard the word "digital currency" and you're now all excited about it. You want to know how to buy and sell digital currencies but don't want to get involved in the world of the cryptic market, where nothing is certain. You are looking for a safe way.

You have found a company that will let you trade in these currencies without any risk, or so you think. This means that you can trade with CFD.

What is CFD?

CFD stands for Contract for Difference. This means that you will be able to speculate on the rise or fall of the currency, or even both, in upcoming deals without having to actually own the currency in question. This means that you can use leverage and open positions. The ability to use leverage when trading CFDs also means that trading with margin is possible.

How does it work?

CFD is a contract between you and your broker. By using this type of trading you will be able to speculate on the rise or fall of the currency, or even both. This means that you won't have to purchase physical currency, but rather contracts tied to them.

What types of CFD are there?

There are two types of CFD for you to choose from: long-term and short-term. The actual financial return associated with these two options will differ but you'll be able to open positions in both of them. The difference between these two types is that for short-term CFDs, the expiration date is usually within a week while long-term CFDs have a more extended expiration date. You can also find spreads listed as well, which are the difference between bid and ask price for each type of contract.

What is leverage?

When trading with a CFD broker, you'll be able to use leverage. Leverage will allow you to open positions by increasing the amount of money that you can use in your trade. This is because it allows you to increase the size of your investment while taking less exposure but if you make a wrong decision, it won't cause the actual loss of assets and have any effect on your bank account.

What is margin?

If you plan to open positions with leverage, it means that you will be able to use margin. Margin, as the name suggests, allows you to borrow funds against the actual value of your assets. In other words, by using margin you can take higher exposure for a certain amount of money. You can also find spreads listed together with your portfolio value and calculated as % towards total value. It's a way of balancing exposure when using leverage.

Each CFD broker will have their own policy regarding leverage. Make sure to check the option before opening positions. This will allow you to find the best brokers that offer leverage and margin.

What is stop loss?

Stop loss is a mechanism built into your trading platform. Once you set up stop loss you won't be able to go beyond it even if the price changes in your favour. It's a way of limiting your losses in case something goes wrong with one of your positions.

What is a broker?

Broker is the middleman between you and the exchange. They will fill your orders, provide you with a trading platform and manage your funds. You'll be able to deposit money with them which they in return will hold as assets until you place a deal. If you open short-term CFDs, it means that you won't have to worry about your broker as there are no expiration dates. Your broker will provide you with a trading platform (an account) where you'll be able to place your orders in the currency that you want.

When do I need to choose a CFD broker?

CFD brokers are free to use, but they are different depending on your needs. You can compare the majority of brokers' features and prices here: How to Choose a Forex Broker?

If you want to use leverage and margin, then you'll need to find a broker that offers these features. Brokers that allow you to open positions with margin are also more expensive than those which don't.

Even if CFD is all about speculation, it's important to choose a broker which will provide you with reliable resources and support when things go wrong. Make sure that you check the list of complaints and reviews for the company that your interested in. This will help when making your decision.

Also be sure to check that you will be able to make withdrawals in the currency in which you've deposited your money. Don't forget that a lot of brokers only provide limited payment options and if they don't accept the currency of your country, you won't be able to place a trade with them.

How do I use it?

When using CFD, all that you'll have to do is compare the current price with the value as entered by yourself in the broker's trading platform. You'll have to compare the current price with the price that you've entered in order to open positions.

If you're using leverage and margin, the process will be a little different. You'll have to calculate how much money you want to open with, for how long and which currency you plan to use. This is usually done by entering your own capital (your investment) as well as your risk capital for each position according to the broker's requirements.

A-Z of Cryptocurrency CFD Trading

Crypto CFDs are derivatives that allow traders to speculate on whether the price of cryptocurrency will go up or down without actually owning any. This is possible because the underlying trade involves leveraging. Basically, you borrow a certain amount of cash (the margin) to buy at what is called a "leverage ratio." When you buy, your profit and loss is based on the difference between what you paid for it and what the market value is when trading closes.

The leverage is determined by the broker who issues the CFD. These exchanges vary around the world in terms of margin requirements, fees, and restrictions on what CFDs can be used for. For example, the biggest global exchange is called and has a leverage ratio of 1-to-100. You can buy any cryptocurrency on that exchange with 1 unit of leverage. On the other hand, a local exchange in Europe called has a leverage ratio of 1-to-5,000. This is one of the reasons why the so many traders have migrated to more competitive exchanges and this has contributed to the dramatic increase in value for Bitcoin and other cryptocurrencies.

US Traders can trade any cryptocurrency on, or while crypto CFDs are available at.

Cryptocurrency CFDs are not subject to SEC regulations but they are subject to Market Regulations Authority (MAR) because they are traded on a clearing account.

CRYPTO TRADING STRATEGIES

The crypto market is at its all-time high in recent times and has attracted unprecedented levels of investment. And because everyone is trying their hand in crypto trading, it can be hard to stand out from the crowd - especially if you're a beginner trader with limited knowledge. But worry not! We've prepared a list of strategies that will give you an edge over your competitors and make your crypto trading journey a lot easier.

Crypto Day Trading Strategies.

What are day trading strategies in the crypto space?

Day trading is a strategy used by traders who want to make money in a short period of time. The aim of day traders is to put on a trade that lasts just a few minutes or less. The great thing about day trading is that you can get in and get out as quickly as possible, so you're able to re-evaluate your strategy and move on to the next trade even faster than usual.

Day trading strategies are incredibly popular due to the fact that they can be successful within very short periods of time. Traders who trade from home, for example, can get in and out of trades in a matter of minutes, whereas traders who trade on a desktop computer must take into account everything that could go wrong with their strategy and how long it would take them to get out of the trade.

If you're new to crypto trading or you're looking for help, we recommend researching your strategy with a background in traditional market methods. Traders who understand the fundamentals of stock trading can adapt this knowledge to their crypto strategies more easily than those who are new to the scene. However, there are all kinds of traders out there who are just using the information you've provided us with and they're making hundreds or even thousands of dollars a day!

Crypto scalping strategies.

Crypto scalping is a strategy used by the majority of day traders. Scalping involves placing a very small position for a very long period of time. It's termed scalping because you are "scalping" prices, and you're only in the market for a short period of time - between 5 to 20 minutes.

Scalpers sell when the price is low and buy when the price is high. With Bitcoin, you can follow the same principle and use it to your advantage.

The first step to using this strategy is to decide what your stop-loss will be and what price level you want to profit at. You can try doing this manually, or you can set a rule for when the price reaches your desired level. For example, if you're trading Bitcoin at $10,000 it makes sense to use a stop-loss of $9000.

Selling at the top is key to using scalping strategies. You can use this strategy as an opportunity to buy low and sell high, and you can make a lot of profit in the process!

Crypto Trend Trading Strategies.

One of the best options when it comes to crypto trading is trading on trends. Traders who trade on trends are known as trend traders and they do well because they're able to take advantage of predictable movements. There are all kinds of traders out there who try to predict technical indicators, and since time is relatively short for crypto traders, you can make a lot of money in that short period of time if you know how to do it correctly.

The most important technical indicators to follow when trading crypto are:

Support and resistance. These are the key levels that indicate where demand and supply are located.

Candlesticks. These are bars that indicate where the price is going to head next and traders use these patterns to predict what the price may be headed towards.

Moving averages. Moving averages are important because they help you predict where the price will end up at and they allow you to create a support or resistance level that predicts this outcome for you.

It's important to remember that it's not always easy to predict trends, so you can't rely solely on technical analysis to make money in the crypto space. However, it is a very important aspect of trading and if you're able to follow these patterns correctly, they can help you make money in the long run.

Crypto Swing Trading Strategies.

Swing trading is another strategy that traders use and it can be extremely profitable. Swing trading is often used by day traders and it involves taking a position in a trade and then moving your position to another market.

Alternatives to swing trading when trading crypto are:

Day trading.

Crypto market making. This involves placing large orders that are usually done manually and using this to take advantage of trends.

Swing traders use similar tools to day traders when it comes to executing their trades. You should also remember that swing traders often also use technical indicators, however swing trading is not just a numbers game. There are all kinds of market factors that can affect your trading strategy and you can't simply rely on technical analysis.

This is why it's important to keep an eye on the overall market when you're trading in the crypto space. You need to make sure that you're in it for the long haul and not just looking to make a quick buck.

Trading Strategies Conclusion

You should be able to spot trends and identify based off of them, this is one of the main benefits of trading crypto. The other benefit is that you can take advantage of rising price levels or falling price levels and be able to capitalize on these short-term movements. Finally, you want to remember that each trade is different and therefore you have to adjust your strategy accordingly.

Mining Crypto

Most of the top cryptocurrencies can be mined, including Bitcoin and Etherium. When you mine crypto, you're taking advantage of a computer's processing power to solve complex mathematical equations. When you solve these equations the computer is rewarded with crypto coins – this is how crypto mining works!

Unfortunately, this activity is no longer as affordable as it was long ago. The more miners have increased and the more bitcoins to be mined have shrunk, the more inconvenient it has become to carry out this activity. Unless you join mining pools.

RISKS MANAGEMENT

Importance of the risk management instruments.

I believe in the importance of risk management instruments in crypto trading.

Risk is defined as a possibility or chance that something does not turn out intended or expected due to uncertain outcome or outcomes. So it's like gambling?

No, it's not like gambling at all! Risk management is just managing your risk for some gain; that's why you can make money if you're good at managing risk.

I will explain the risks of crypto trading to you, when I think of them.

The first risk that I think of in crypto trading is: Losing your money (It sounds like gambling, but it's not). This is the risk that you take in a gamble. If you play the game with good and bad luck, then you might win or lose your money.

It's different with a well-managed risk management system. To use an example, you can start with $100. If you manage to earn $10 every day for 100 trading days, then you will have $1000. It's a well-managed risk management system, and not gambling.

Is losing your money the only risk in crypto trading?

No, it's not the only risk in crypto trading; there is more than one risk. Now I will explain to you what other risks are in crypto trading. First I will explain to you the risk of losing your investment.

The second risk is the risk of losing money when you lose a certain amount of money. In a sense, this is very similar to losing your investment. For example, you invest $1000 and after 10 days it goes down to $500. That is a loss of $500, but it's actually losing your investment. If you have more than one investment, then I recommend that you follow a certain percentage to set yourself up. I believe that 40% of your investment should be in one asset. And after that, spread it over five assets to get the best results.

The third risk is the risk of losing money when you lose your deposit in any way. In a sense, this is very similar to losing money after losing money. For example, you put a deposit of $1000 and after 20 days, it's lost.

The fourth risk is the risk of losing money when you lose some or all of your investment. For example, you invest $500 and after 10 days it goes down to $0. This is losing some or all of your money.

You can use the first, second and third risks in your favor with a well-managed risk management system. The fourth risk is really a risky business if you do not know what you're doing. I will explain to you why.

The fourth risk is a risk because you might lose some of your investment in crypto trading. You can also lose all of your investment if you do not know what you're doing. It's like gambling in this respect. If you do not know what you're doing, then it could end up costing you more money than just losing your investment!

When there is no risk management, then there is a higher chance that the whole investment will be lost, especially when you use leverage to trade with. I will explain to you how you can control this risk.

The fifth risk is the risk of losing your money if crypto trading goes bad in anyway. This is the risk of return-less investment. If crypto trading ends badly, then your money can also end up being lost in that process.

The risks of trading cryptocurrencies are mostly related to volatility. Cryptocurrencies are high-risk speculative products, and, as said before, it is important to understand the risks before you start trading.

All the risks considered are due to the following causes:

Volatility: unexpected changes in market sentiment can lead to sudden fluctuations in price. It is quite common for the value of cryptocurrencies to quickly plummet by hundreds, if not thousands of dollars.

Absence of regulation: at the moment, cryptocurrencies are not regulated by either governments or central banks.

Risk of technical error and hacking: there is no fool proof way to prevent technical problems, human error or hacking activities.

Risk of forks and disruptions: trading cryptocurrencies involves additional risk such as hard forks or disruptions. It is important to be well aware of these risks before trading on these products. When a hard fork occurs, there could be a lot of volatility around that event and this could heavily affect the cryptocurrency price.

How to manage the 5 risks

The ones considered before are the five main risks of investing in crypto trading, but there are more than five risks in all types of investment! It's different for every person because every person has their own way to do things. I will explain to you how risk management helps you with this different way of doing things.

If you use a well-managed risk management system, then I recommend that you have the best possible results in your investment.

So let's start with introducing the key points of risk management.

You can start with: The first five risks of crypto trading and managing them properly. The first risk is losing your investment (It's the same as if you gamble). The second risk is losing money when you lose a deposit. The third risk is losing money when you lose a certain amount of money. The fourth risk is losing money when your deposit goes wrong. And the fifth risk is a possible loss of money when crypto trading goes wrong.

You can use these five risks in your favor with a well-managed risk management system. If you use it to lose your money, then it's not useful at all. You can also win in that way, but I wouldn't recommend that you do so.

Risks of trading cryptocurrencies with CFDs

There is a series of risks that are linked to a particular form of crypto trading: trading with CFDs

Trading with CFDs exposes you to multiple risks that are, however, different than when you buy these cryptocurrencies directly.

CFDs, as mentioned, are high-risk speculative products. As explained above, in CFD trading you only need to deposit a small percentage of the total value of the trade to open a position. Profits and losses are based on the total value of the trade. The volatility of cryptocurrencies, combined with trading on margin, could cause significant losses.

CFDs carry a considerable risk of Slippage or Gap. In fact, volatility can cause prices to move from one level to another, without passing through the intermediate level. This usually occurs during periods of high volatility. As a result, a stop loss order may be executed at a level worse than the client requested. This can make losses highly worse.

The costs of CFDs may also be higher than on other asset classes, while the price variation, compared to real or traditional currencies, can be very significant and consequently affect the determination of the value of CFD positions.

Make sure you fully understand the risks associated with this product before you start trading. Only invest if you are an experienced investor with an excellent understanding of the financial markets. This form of trading is not suitable for everyone. For this reason, we recommend seeking the advice of an independent financial advisor before deciding whether to start trading CFDs.

The Financial Conduct Authority (FCA) regulates CFDs. This means that companies offering CFDs on cryptocurrencies must be licensed and supervised by the FCA. Individual complaints can be directed to specific competent authorities (the Financial Ombudsman Service (FOS) for the UK) and eligible consumer clients have access to the Financial Services Compensation Scheme

(FSCS). However, these protections do not offer any compensation for losses related to trading activity.

MYTHS AND FALSE BELIEFS ABOUT CRYPTOCURRENCIES

In short, it seems that those who have never invested in cryptocurrencies have made a serious mistake. In the past but also for the future this really presents itself as a very appetizing opportunity not to be missed.

Especially from the speculative aspect, cryptocurrencies can give a lot because they grow very quickly and have very large fluctuations, but as always, before being able to invest in them you need to know them better otherwise everything could only be reduced to the classic waste of time and money and you don't want to. that this happens right? Well then let's find out together all the inaccuracies that are said about what concerns the investment in cryptocurrencies and especially about 3 important projects such as: ethereum, bitcoin and litecoin.

Cryptocurrencies are just an economic bubble

Believing that it is just a bubble destined to burst is a very common mistake that discourages investing in cryptocurrencies because one is convinced that this market has no interest and no prospect. But by now those who know the sector a little know well what great movement and interest have generated cryptocurrencies worldwide in people such as developers, miners, traders or people like you who want to invest in business and dreamers who aspire to see a free world. from the rigid and sometimes tyrannical control of the banks. Bitcoin and other cryptocurrencies, in fact, are free currency, not subject like the classic currency to the strict regulations and controls of the Central Banks.

The fact that it is not a bubble is demonstrated by the case of Ethereum.

The Enterprice Ethereum Alliance is one of the most important and influential multinational organizations in the world that includes industries, oil companies, gas companies, as well as software developers such as Micrsosoft. All of them have just officially launched a

73

project dedicated to the development of Ethereum! It will therefore be the case to consider Ethereum and start investing in it, what do you say?

Cryptocurrencies are not very widespread and used

Another commonplace to dispel is precisely this. What many say is that investing in cryptocurrencies would be not very convenient and risky because it is a little liquid and not very widespread asset, therefore little used. But if this is true how do they manage to break through the roofs they had previously achieved in terms of value?

Bitcoins have gone from a few dollars in value in a few years to an average value of 7,000 each (peaks close to the 20,000 dollars recorded at the end of 2017). This is proof of the great potential of these currencies, plus it is known that transactions are generated in the world with virtual currencies for hundreds of millions of dollars.

The big advantage is also the complete anonymity and freedom from the interbank system which pushes more and more people to use bitcoins.

Investing in cryptocurrencies is complicated and not for everyone

This is the third and final misconception to dispel and there are many reasons why we should never listen to rumors of this type, risking to miss the opportunity to invest in a big business that is taking off. In reality, both mining cryptocurrencies and buying them today is a rather simple operation. But the best thing to do is trading on cryptocurrencies through CFDs to be carried out directly online and it is certainly the activity with the highest profit margins.

The first thing to do is to understand the systems that are currently available and find good and proven trading techniques, then the strong fluctuations typical of virtual currency markets will take care of it to make profits skyrocket. Of course, however, it cannot be said to be a walk in the park, you need to study a lot to understand how to apply the best tactics and undertake the right market trends, with the patience and prudence to get out of it at the right time

CONCLUSION

To invest in cryptocurrencies and on the new records set by virtual currencies in the latest online quotes, it is important to understand above all what we are talking about by understanding how it works. In fact, we are talking about digital currencies and realities such as Bitcoin, Ethereum, Litecoin, Monero and Ripple, which record interesting results in this period and which can also be considered for important investment opportunities. Buying cryptocurrencies today is very simple and involves two important roads such as Exchanges or online CFD trading brokers.

With the Exchanges solution, important advantages are accessed such as the direct purchase of the aforementioned digital currencies with low commission costs by platforms that are now well known and consolidated in the sector such as Binance, Coinbase, Bitpanda and others.

Investing with online trading brokers, on the other hand, means using contracts for difference and operating with respect to the price trend of digital currencies even in the case of high volatility. Also in this case the commission costs are very low and useful tools such as free demo account and platform with web access are almost always provided to invest more immediately in the best cryptocurrencies.

What are the 5 cryptocurrencies in which to invest in the next few years? Well looking at the latest numbers, there are currently interesting quotes on Bitcoin, Ethereum, Ripple, Litecoin and Monero that can be traded on Exchanges or CFD brokers.

So you just have to start: read up, read, study and then do a lot of practice on demo accounts. And at that point ... join the fray!

www.ingramcontent.com/pod-product-compliance
Lightning Source LLC
Chambersburg PA
CBHW061701240326
41458CB00154B/1417

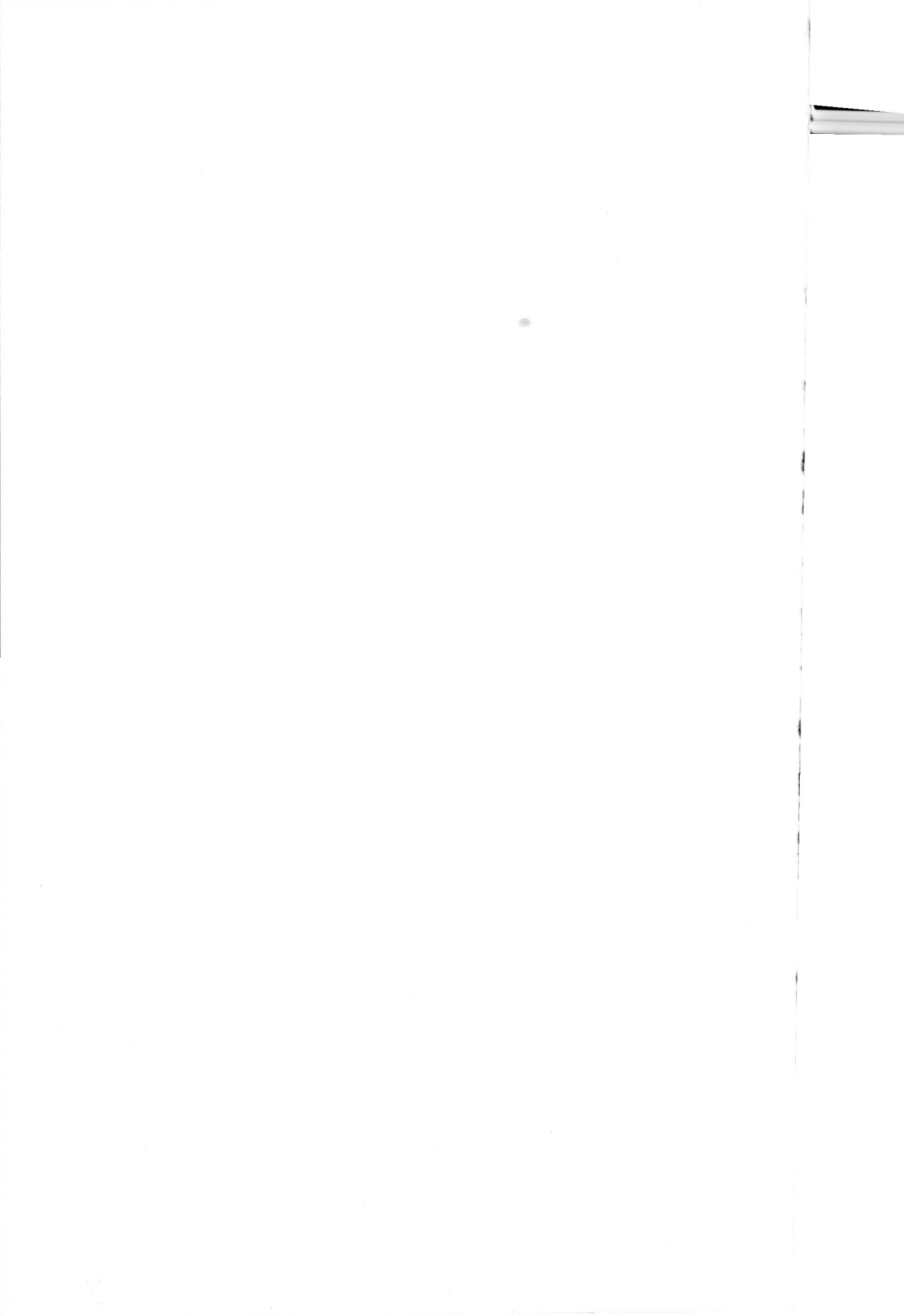